Yorkie Spirit
Adult Coloring Book
An Exploration of the Indomitable Yorkshire Terrier

It's a Yorkie Life

ISBN-13: 978-0692516898
ISBN-10: 0692516891

DEDICATION

To all Yorkie lovers, big and small.
And to the Yorkies that inspired it all: Mickey and Chloe,
and their best friends: Ezra and Jack.

ACKNOWLEDGEMENT

Thank you to the following publications for the "spirit" component of these designs:

- Annie & Oliver (Horapollo, Cousin, Du Pre, & Ruelle, 1574, p. 156)
- Archie (Ward & Griffith, 1902, p. 150)
- Baby (Jasper & Pimgadie, 1912, p. 245)
- Bailey (Washburn & Co & Henry G. Gilbert Nursery and Seed Trade Catalog Co, 1869, p. 53)
- Bella (Childs & Collection, 1914, p. 128)
- Bruno (Snyder, n.d.)
- Chloe (Goodrich, 1845, p. 158)
- Daisy (H.W. Koerner, Koerner, & Henry G. Gilbert Nursery & Seed Trade Catalog, 1900, p. 78)
- Emma (Hooker, 1830-1833, p. 458)
- Ezra (Dodge, 1873, p. 93)
- Gracie (Ricci & Sara Anderson Galleries, Inc., 1915, p. 78)
- Heidi (Herbert, 1868, p. 293)
- Jack (Hood & Shepherd, 1881, p. 580)
- Jake (Figuier & Gillmore, 1869, p. 435)
- Lady (Pollard & Pollard, 1902, p. 264)
- Lucky (Bass, 1900, p. 16)
- Maddie (Sears, Roebuck and Co., 1916, p. 214)
- Max (W & Mulready, 1883, p. 20)
- Milo (Elton, 1854, p. 35)
- Molly (various, 1902, p. 506)
- Penny (The Craftsman, 1901, p. 374)
- Rusty (Ball, 1891, p. 235)
- Sammy (Crabtre, 1874, p. 39)
- Scout (Alpine Club London & Ball, 1859, p. 192)
- Simon (Kipling & Willeumier, 1895, p. 221)
- Teddy (Moore, 1884, p. 150)
- Toby (Horapollo, Cousin, Du Pre, & Ruelle, 1574, p. 72)

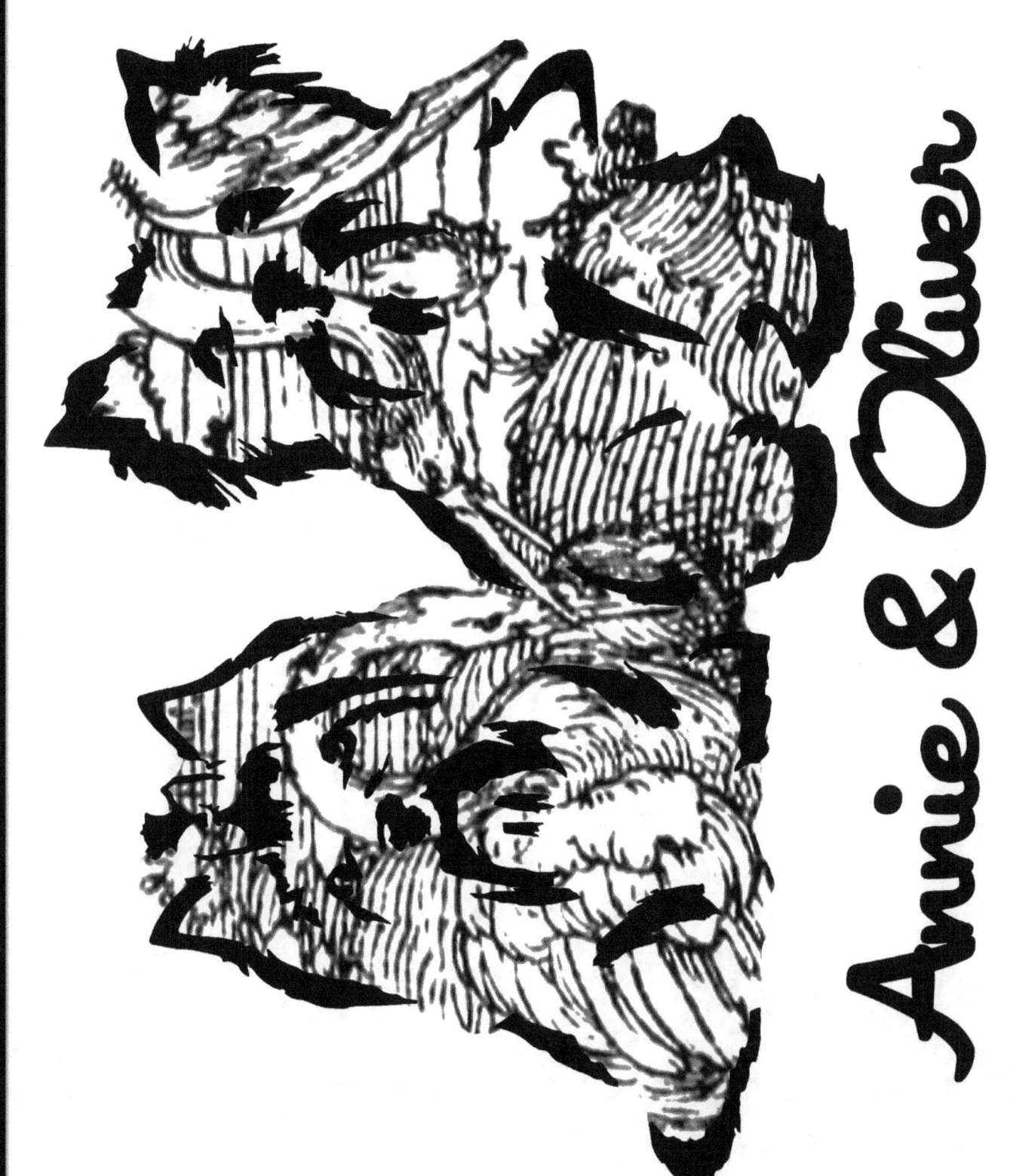

Annie & Oliver

Yorkie Spirit Adult Coloring Book

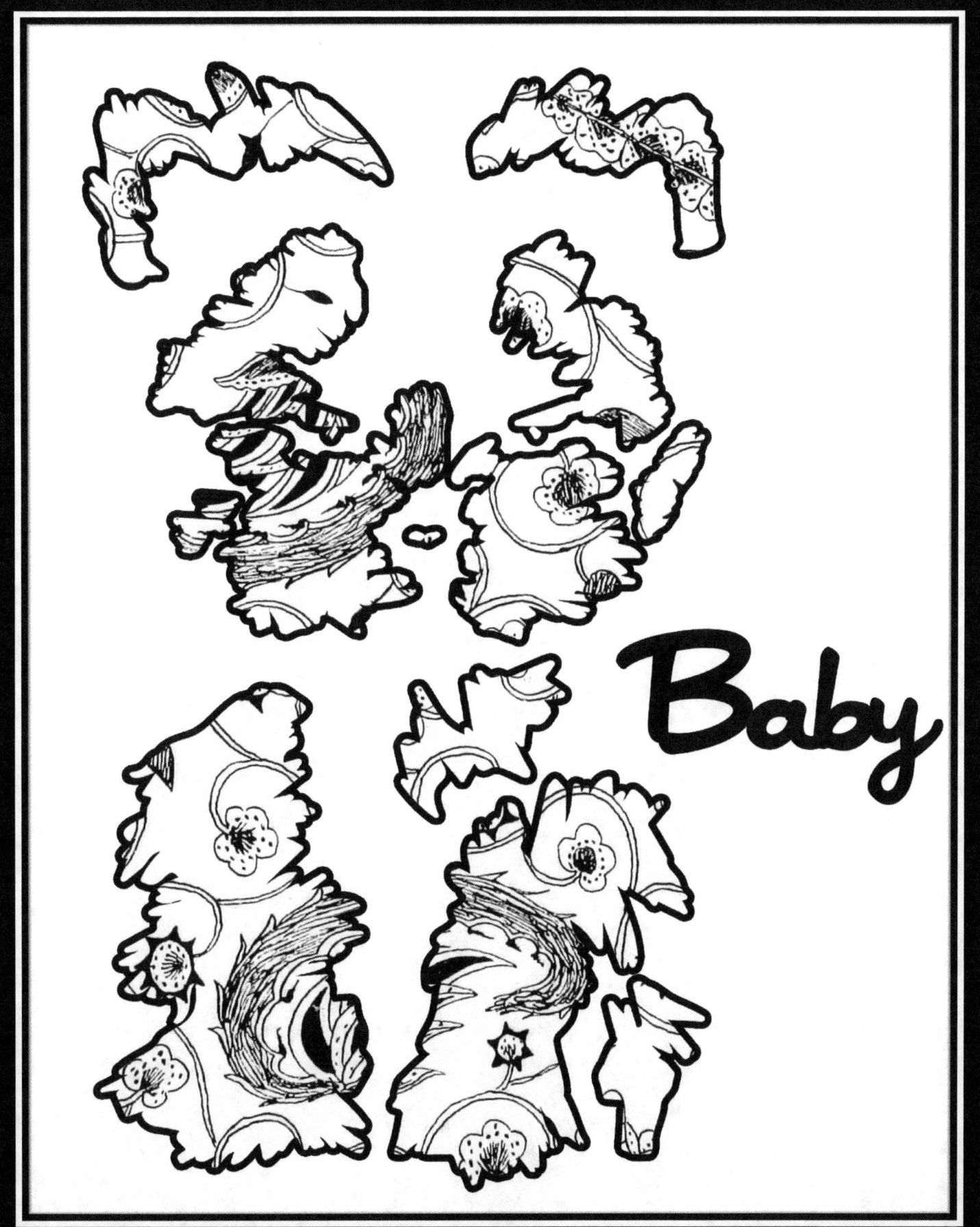

Baby

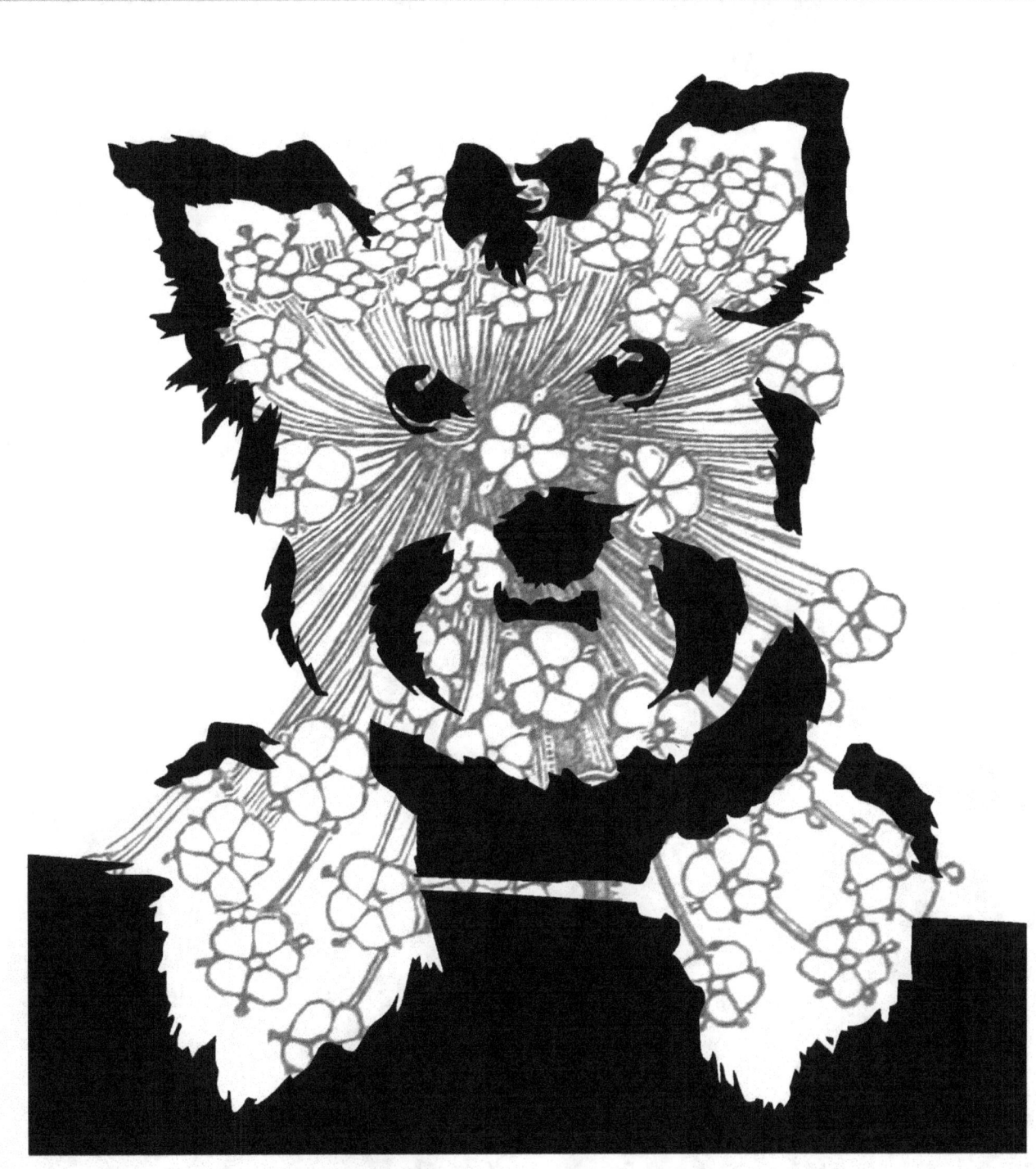

Bailey

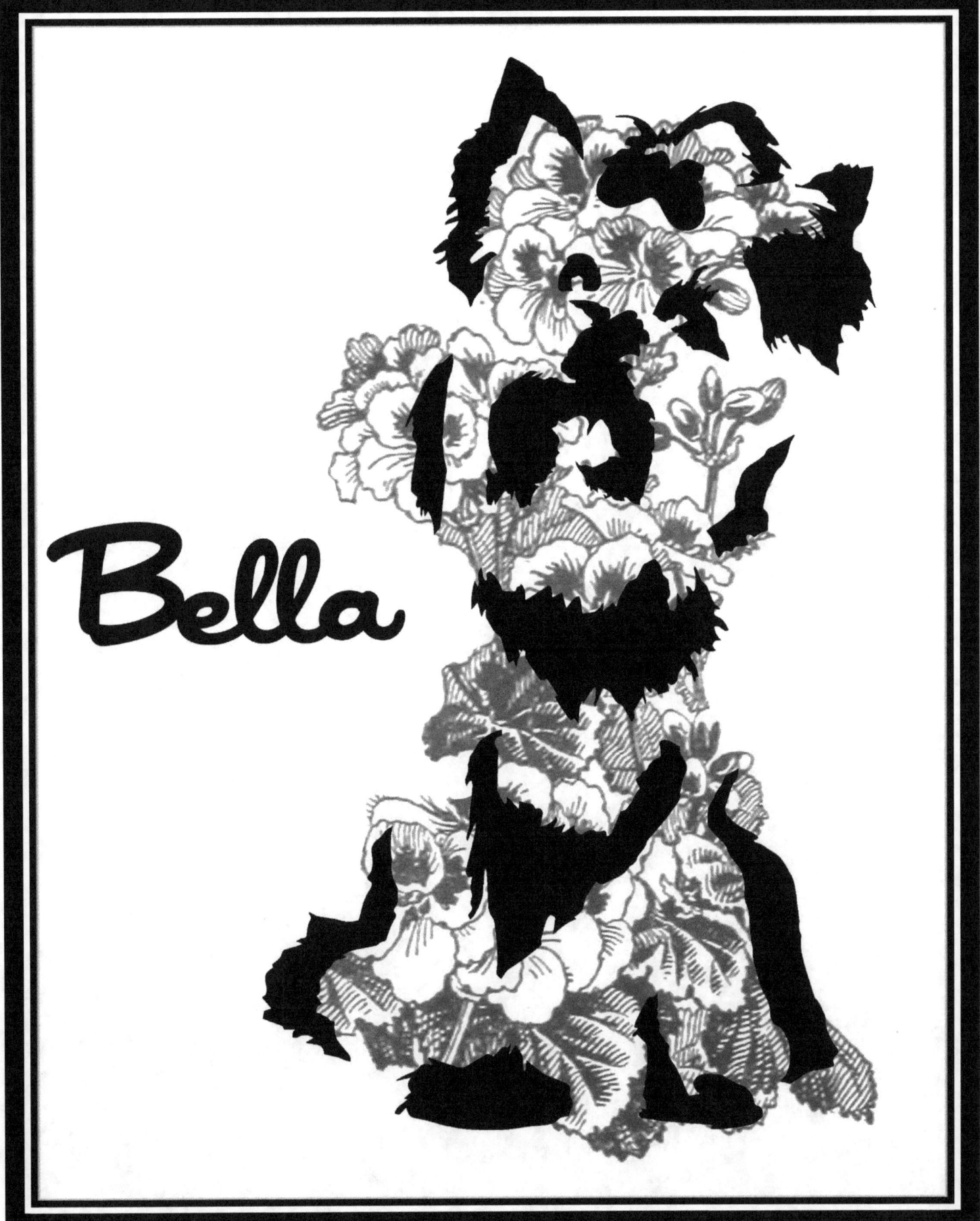

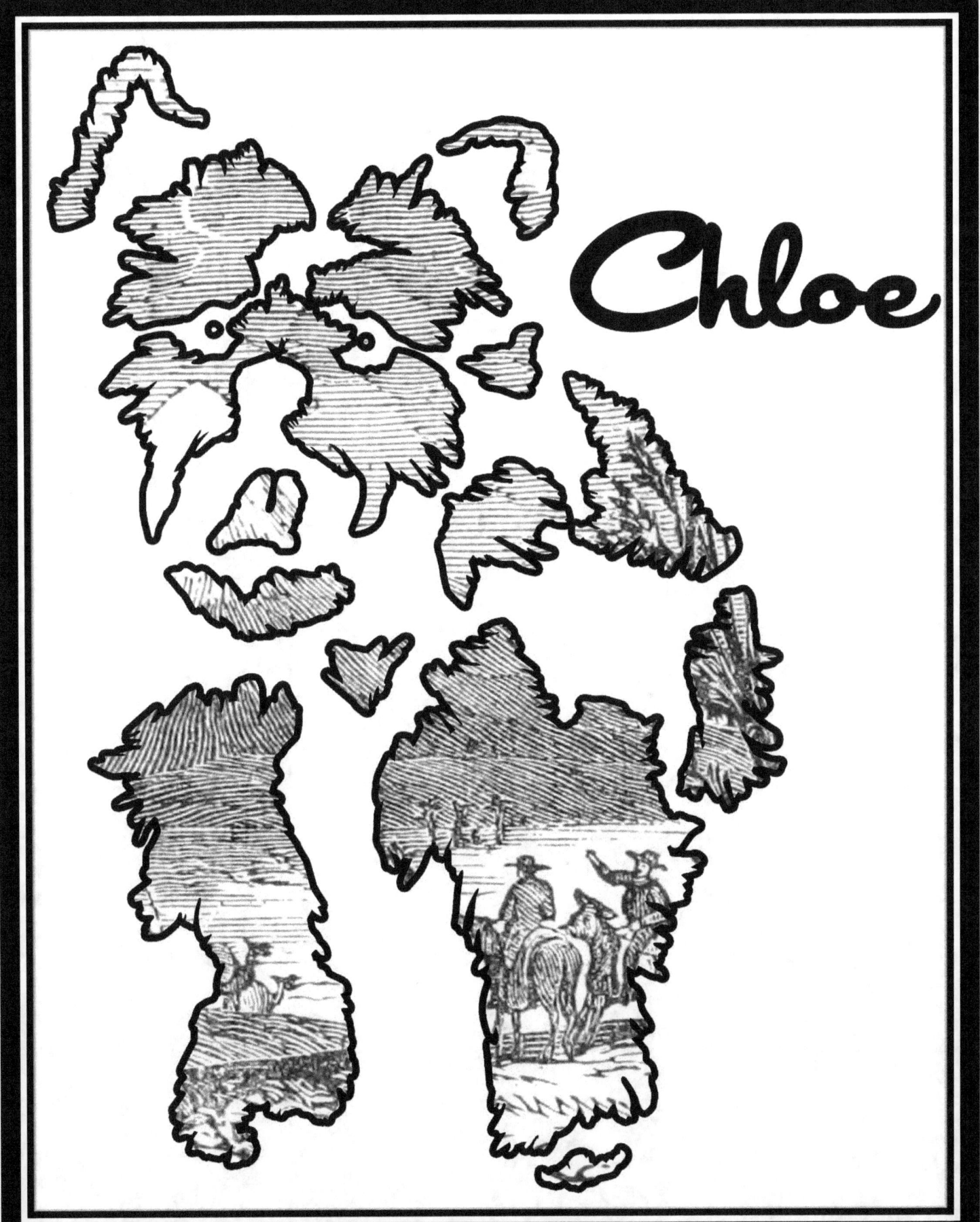

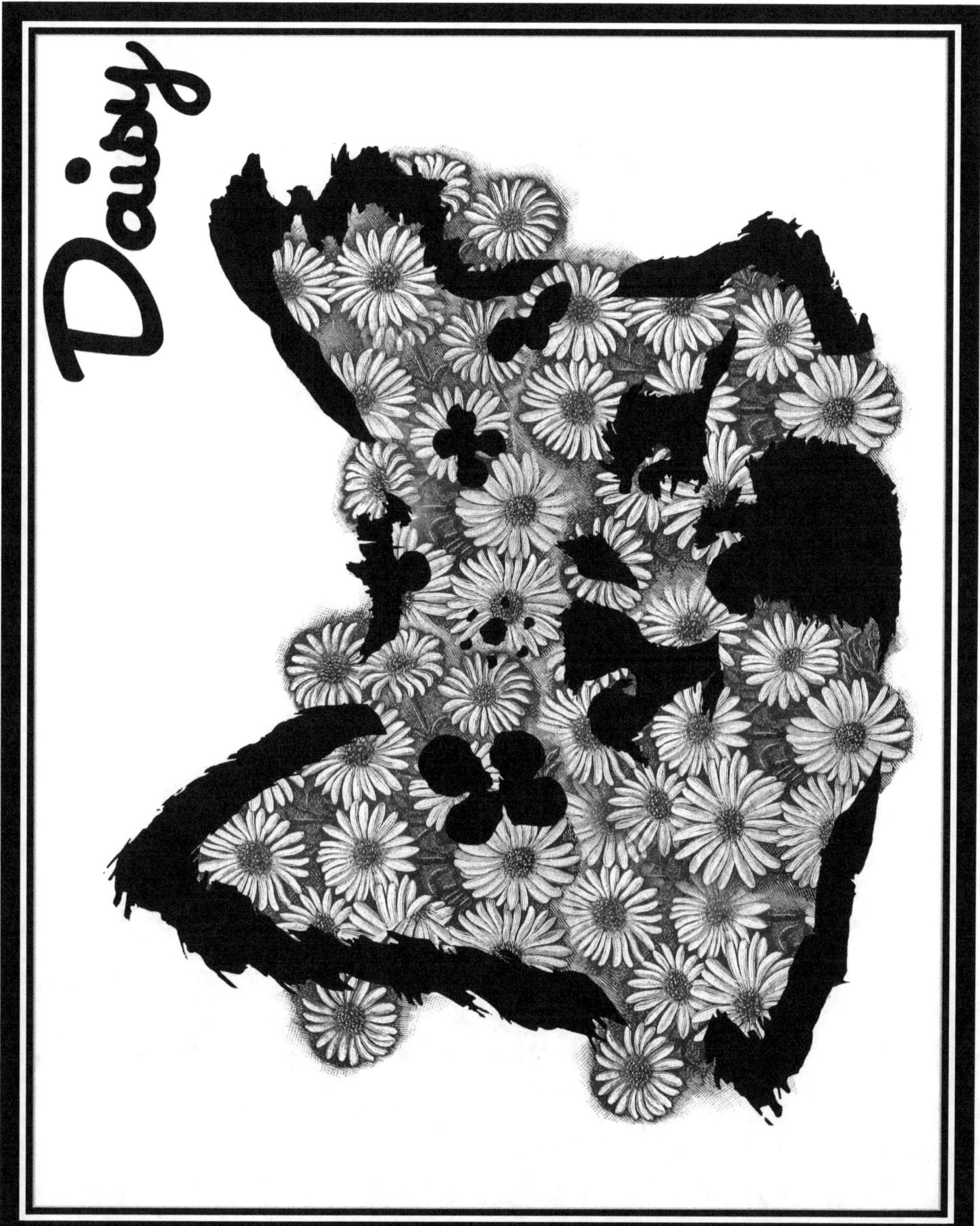

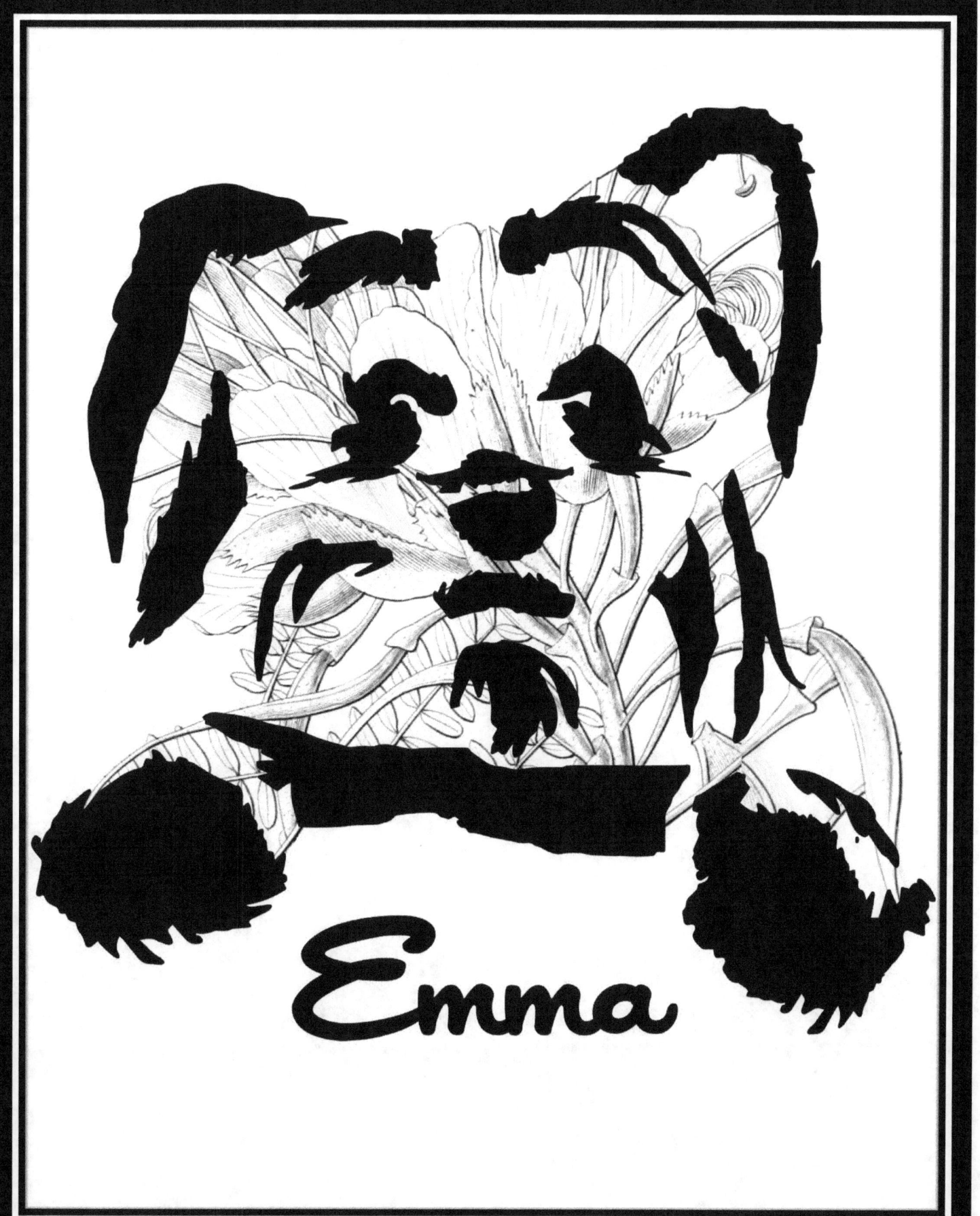

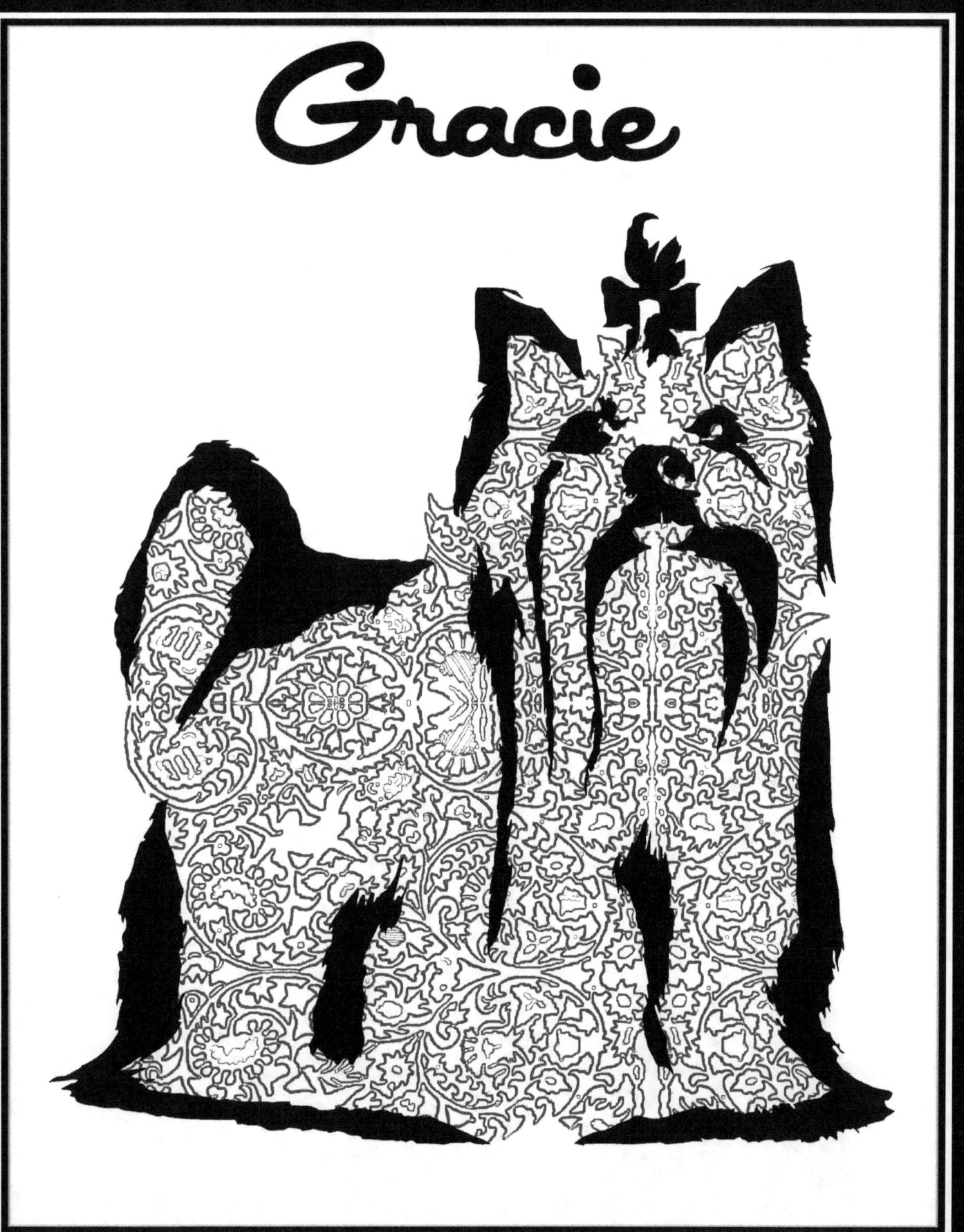

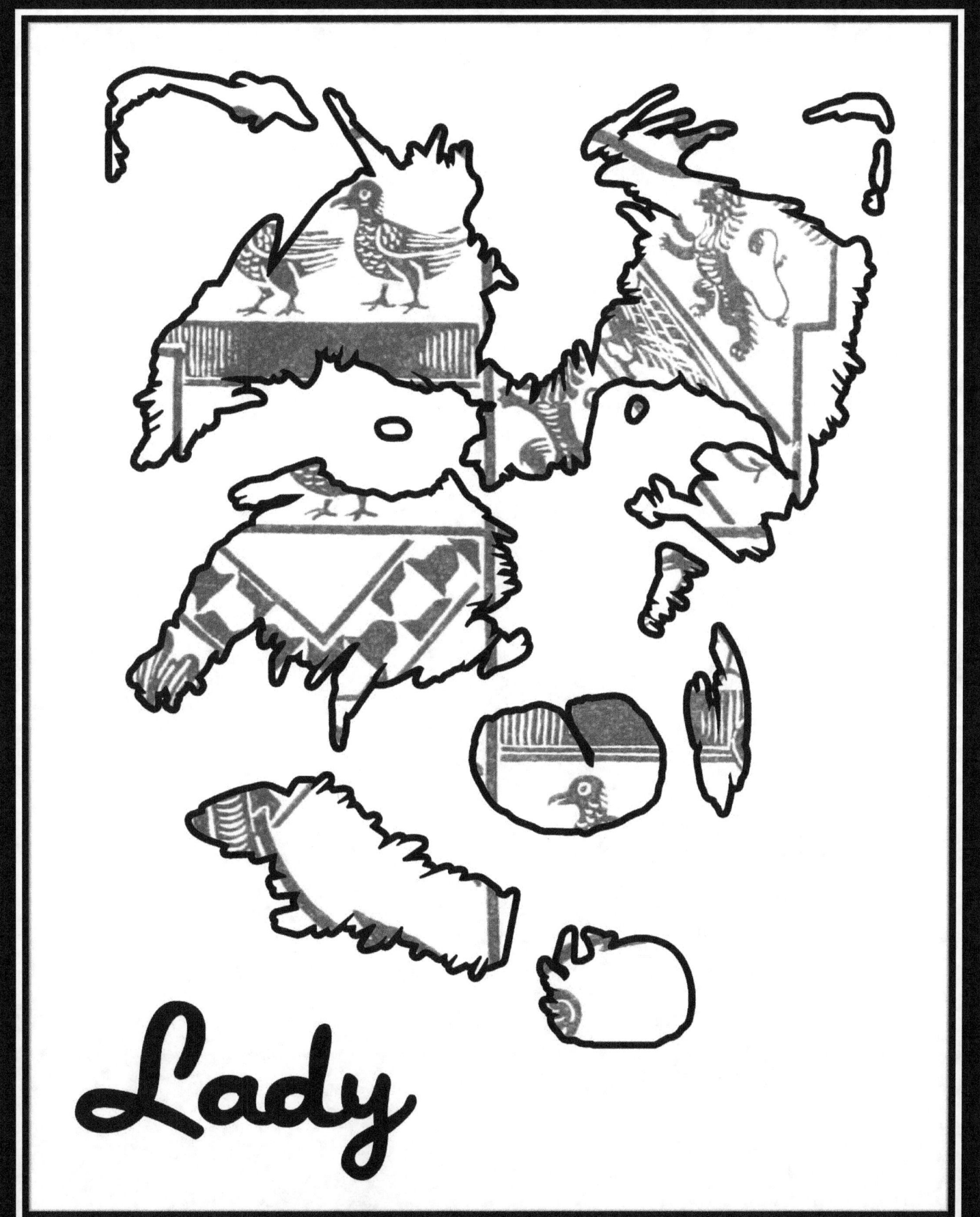

Lady

Yorkie Spirit Adult Coloring Book

Maddie

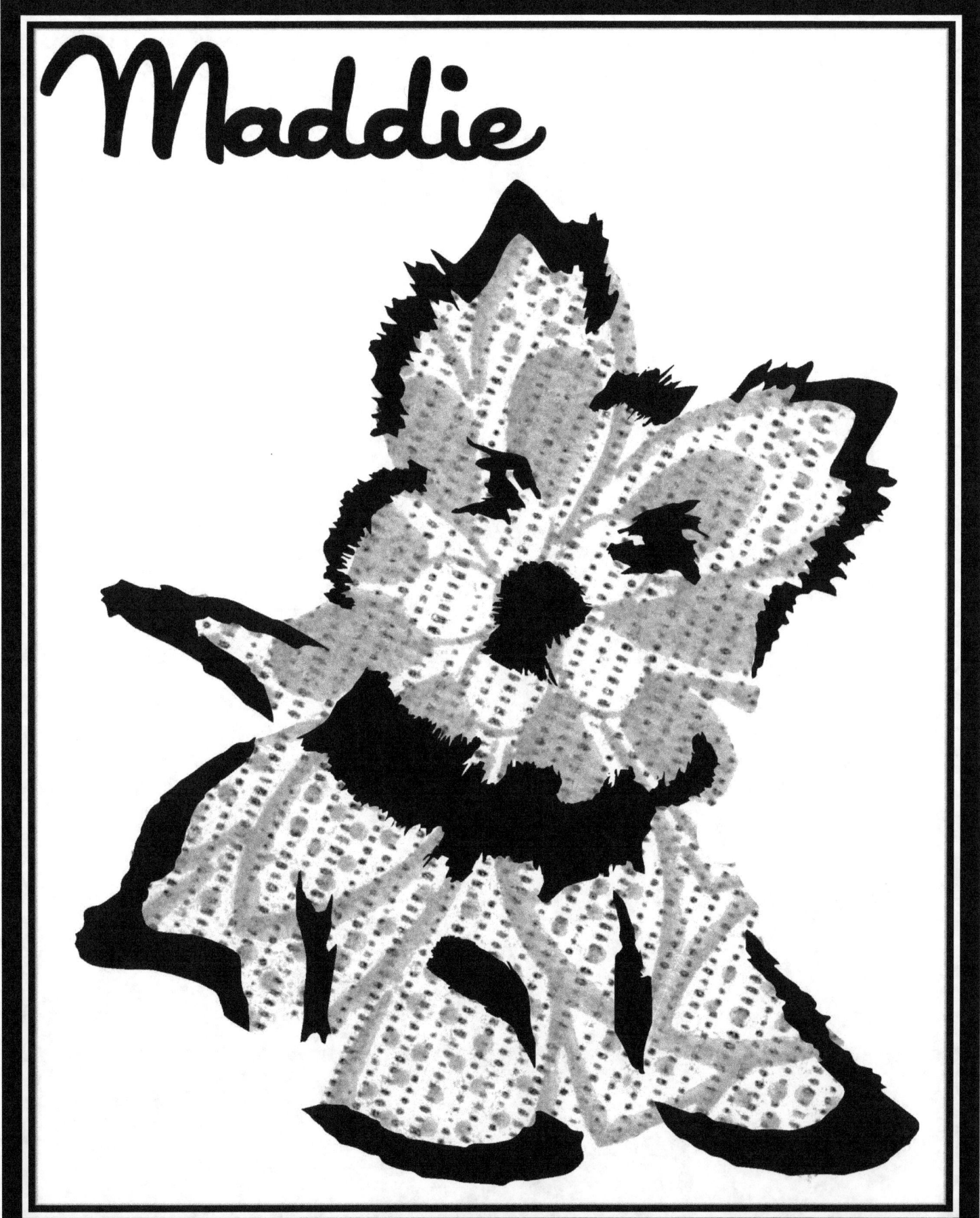

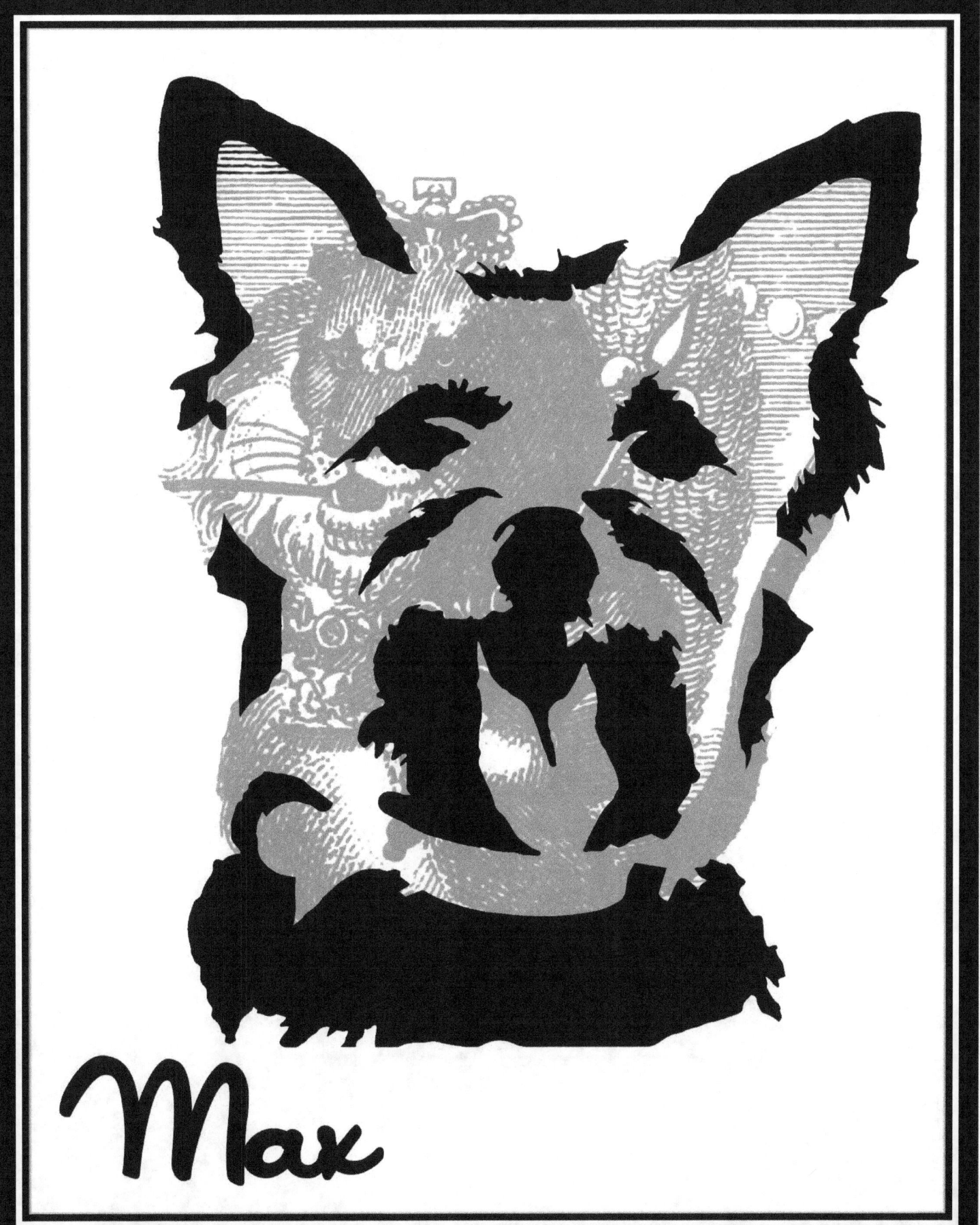

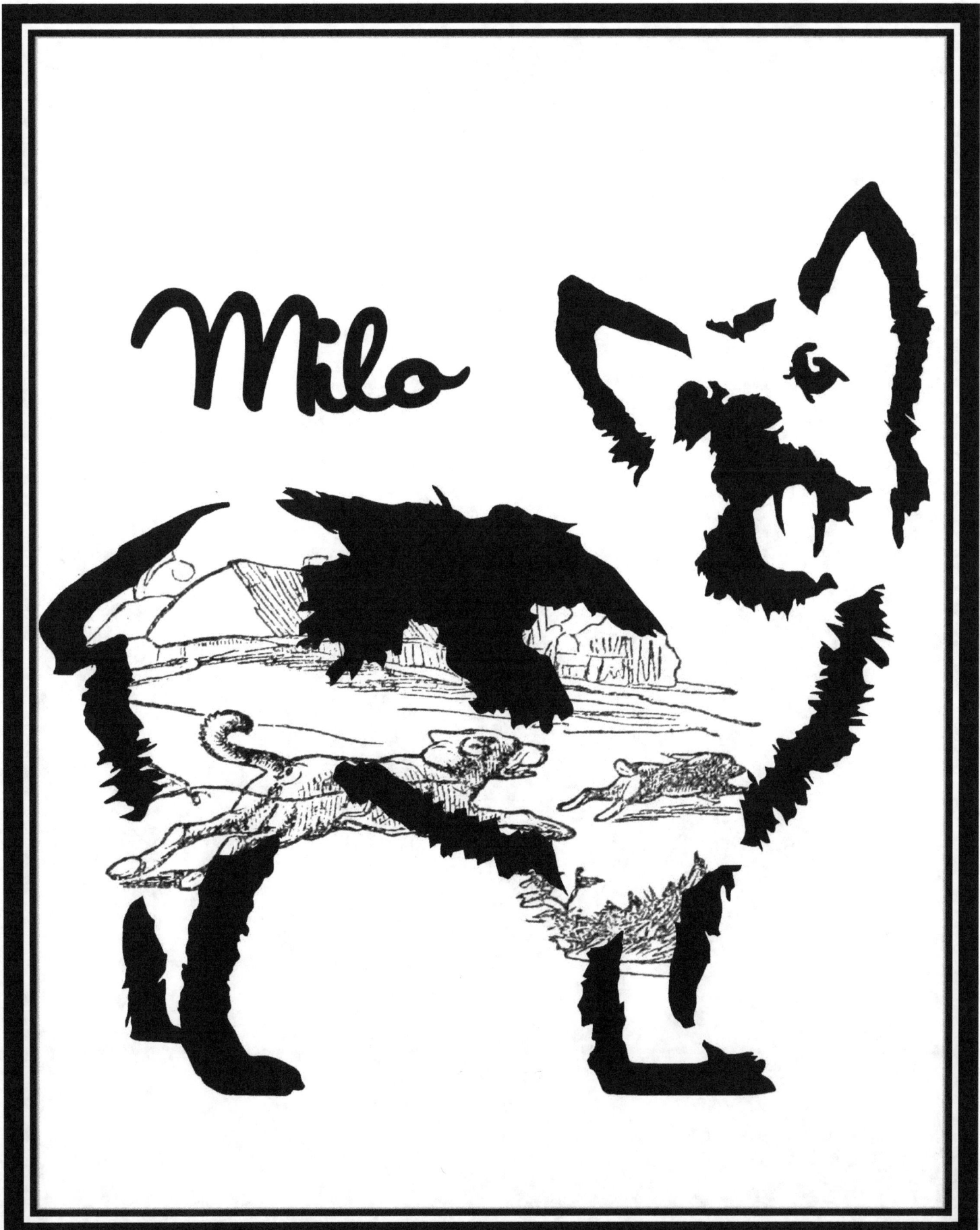

Milo

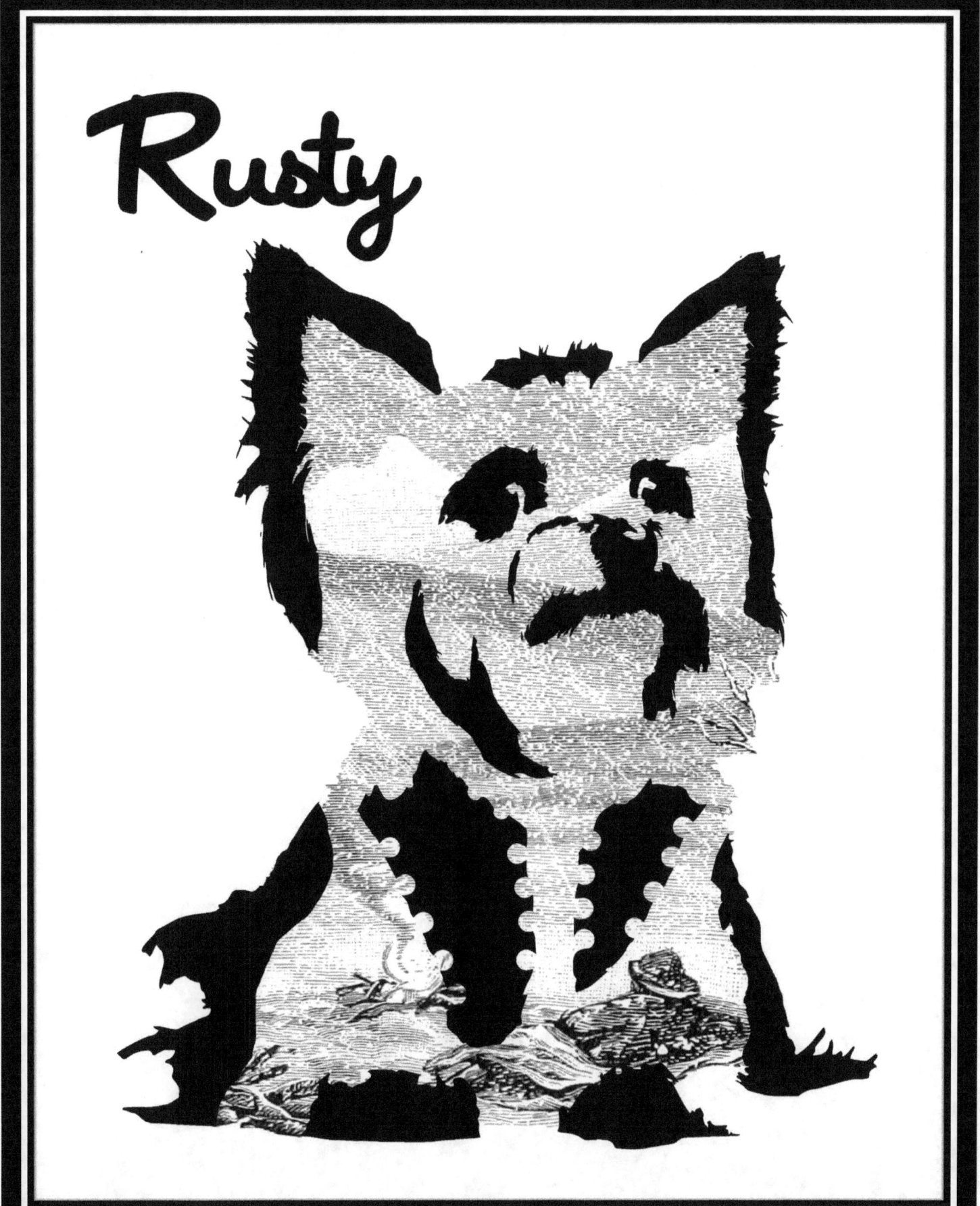

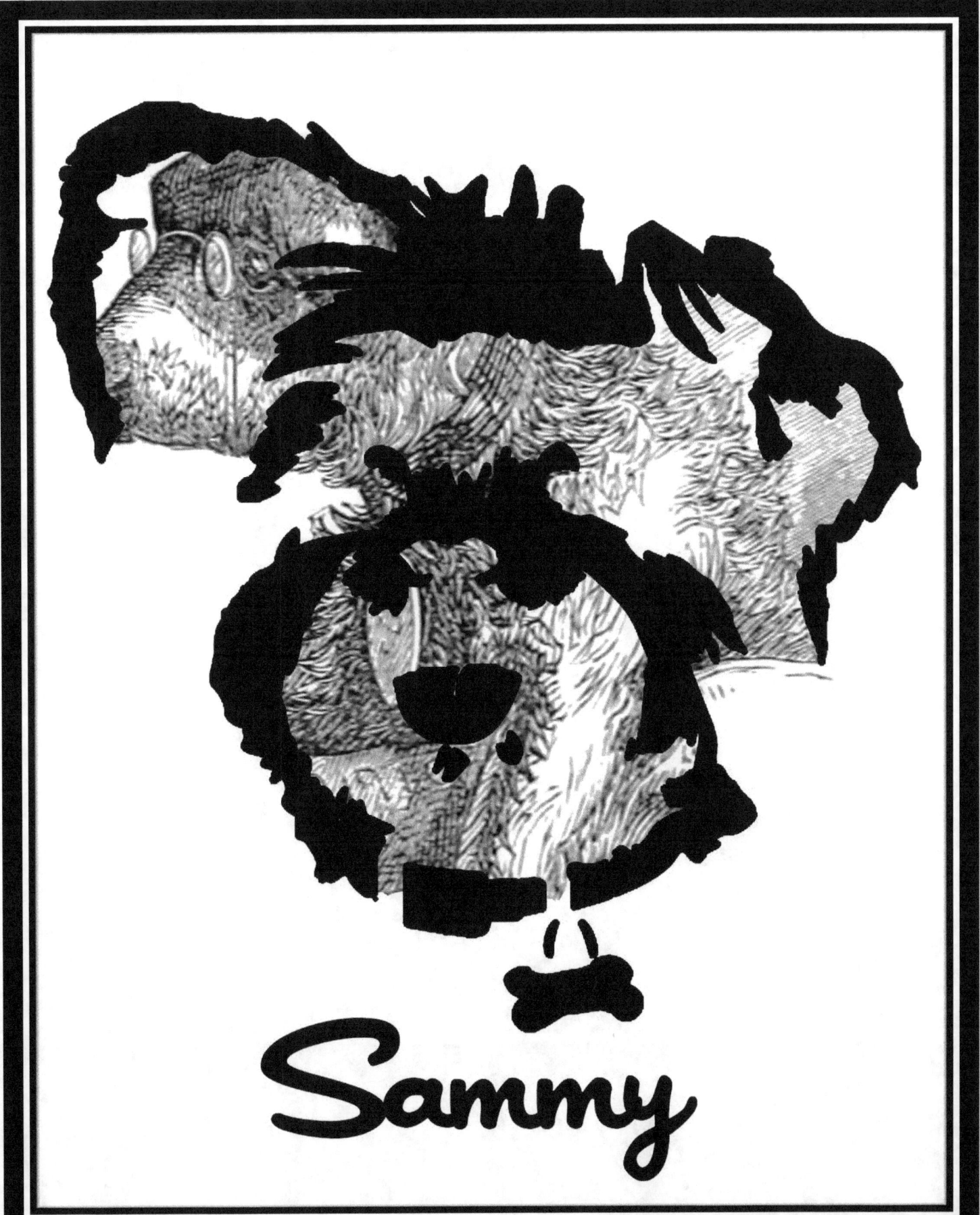

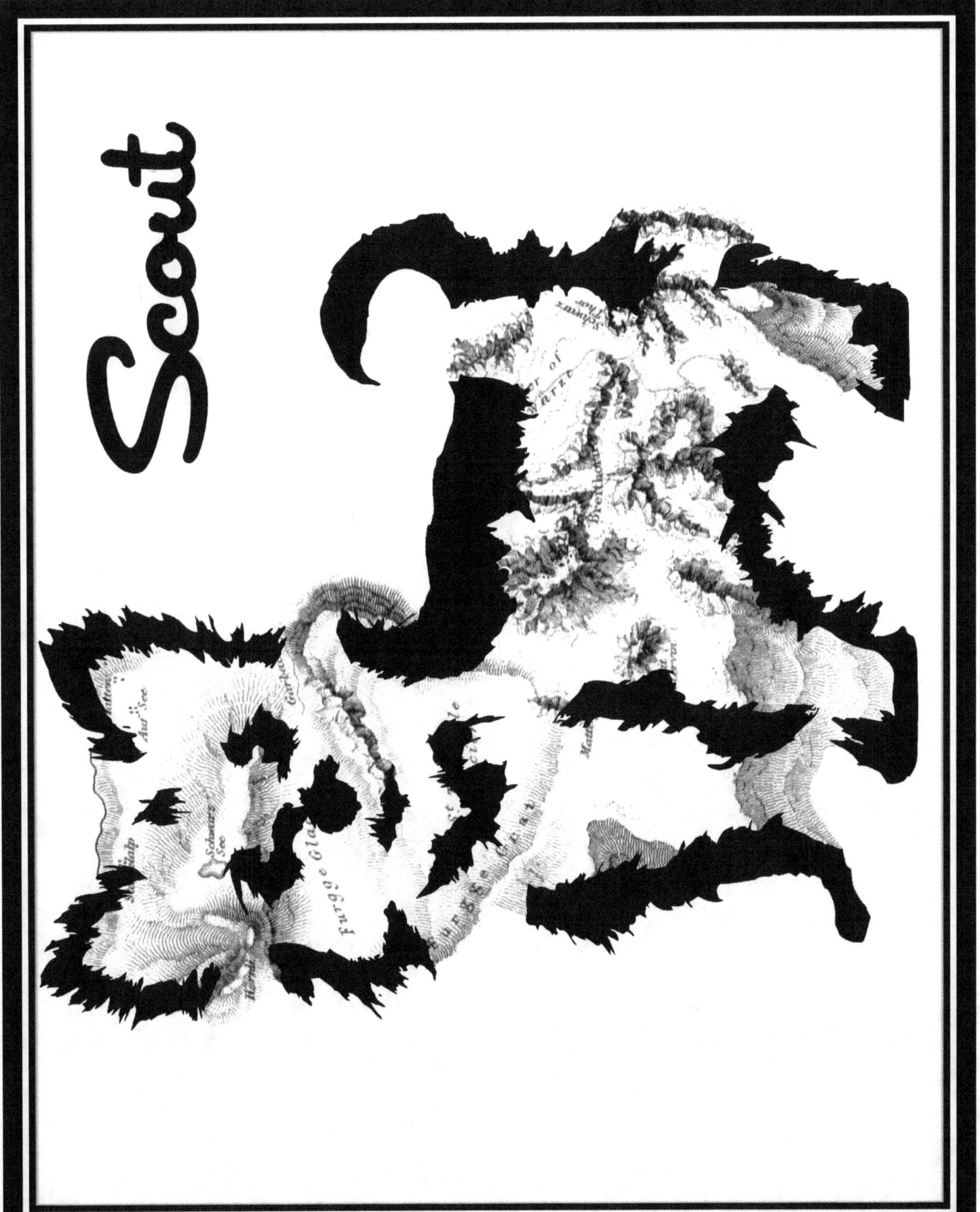

Simon

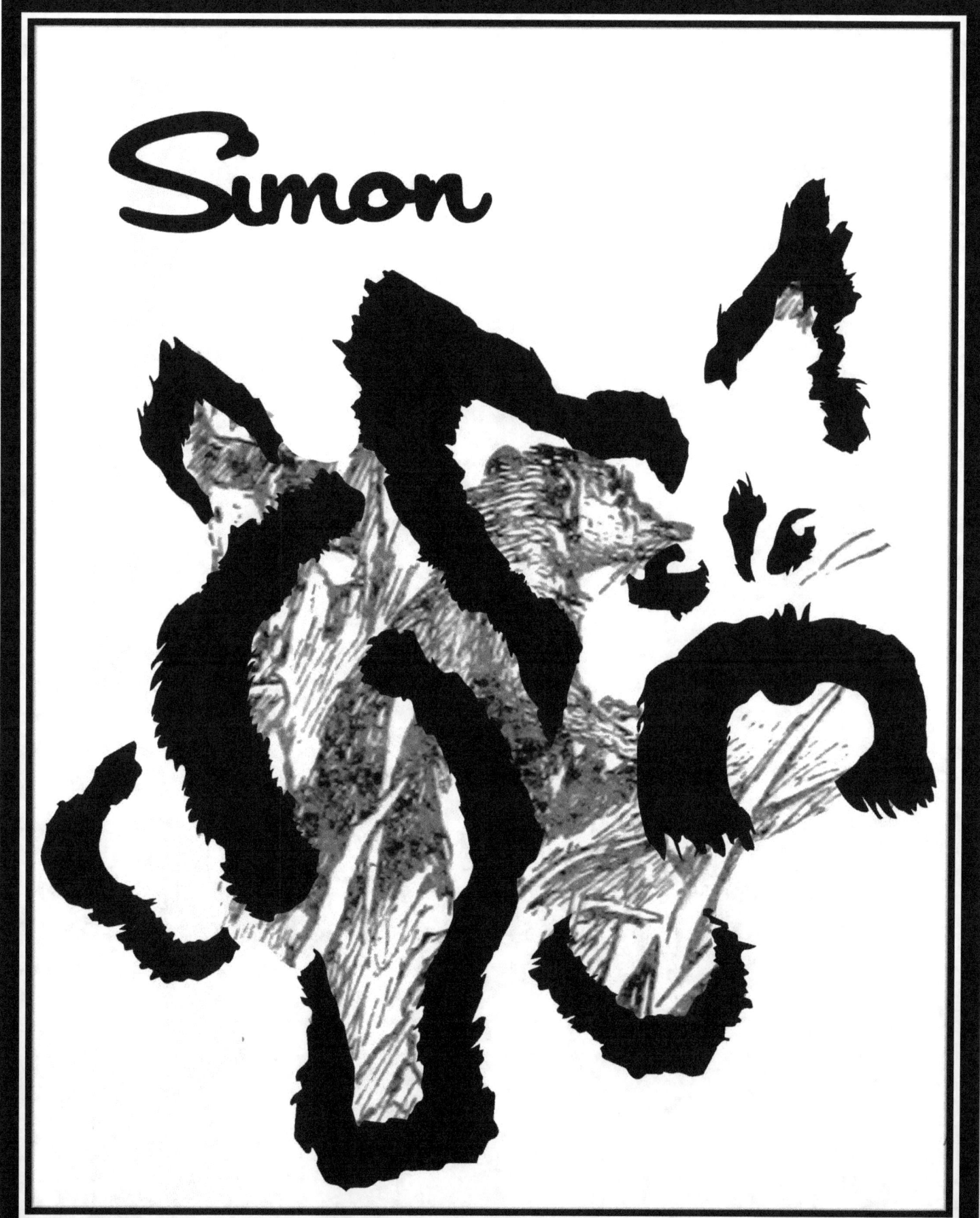

Teddy

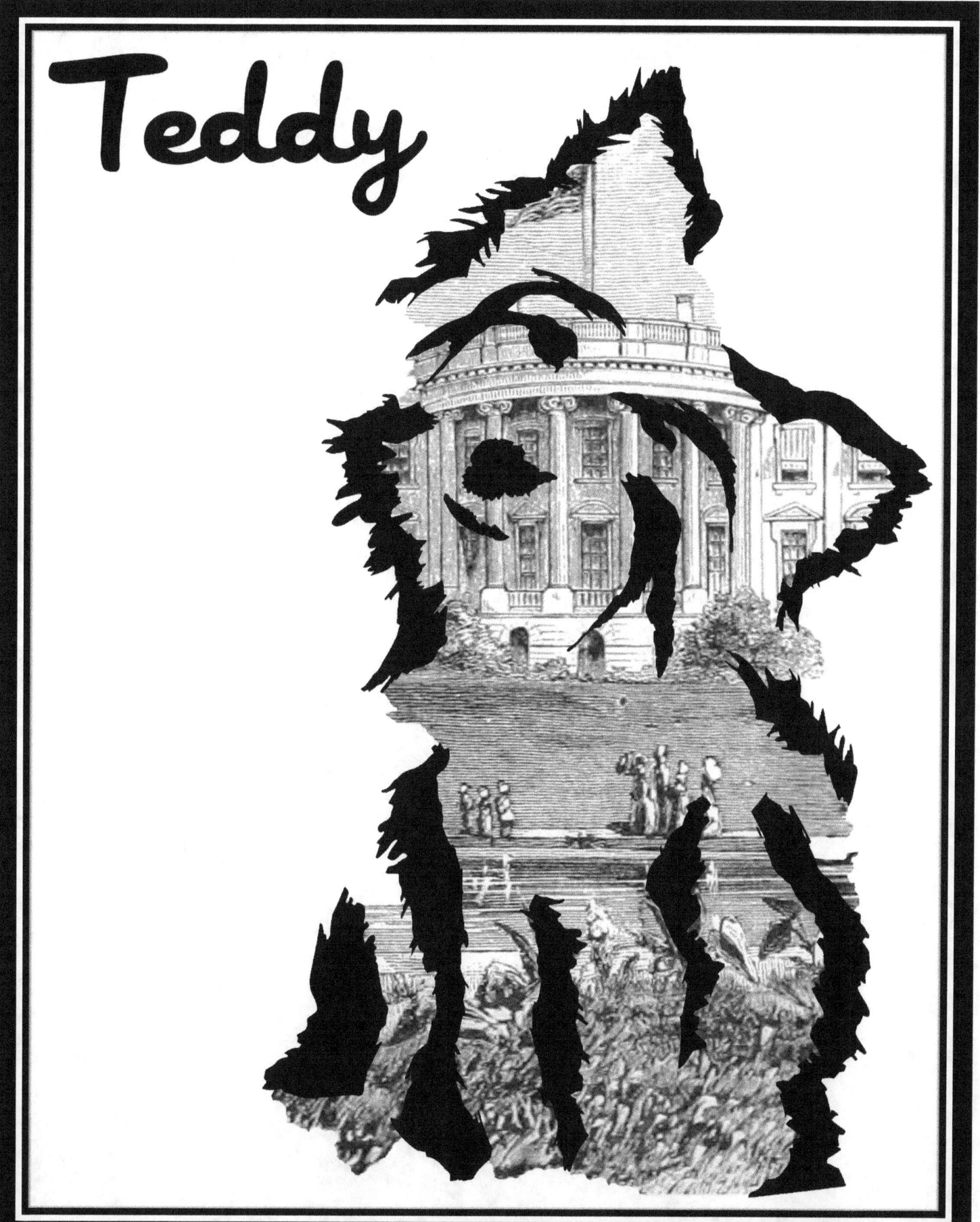

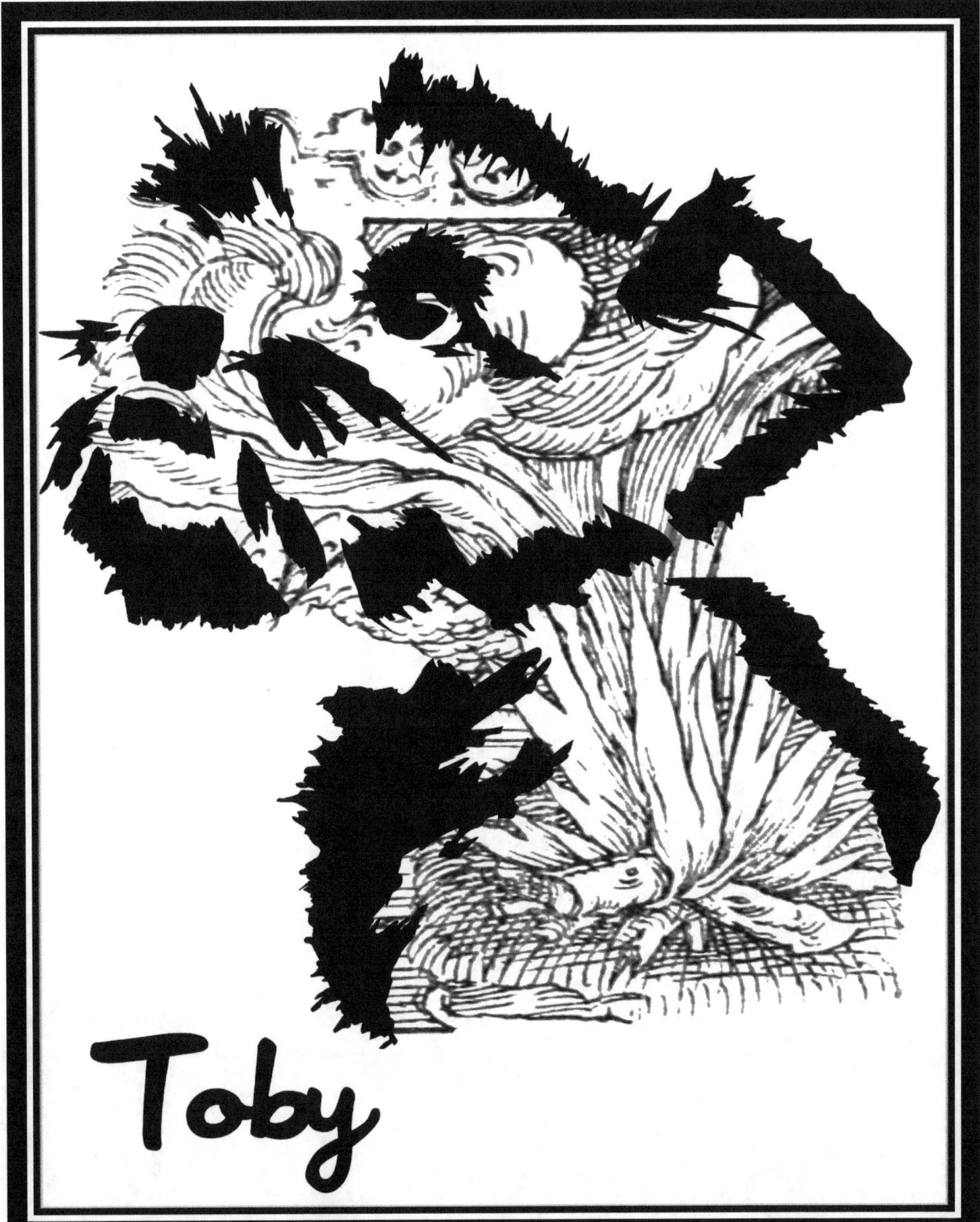

Toby

BIBLIOGRAPHY

Alpine Club London, & Ball, J. (1859). *Peaks, Passes, and Glaciers. A series of excursions by members of the Alpine Club. Edited by J. Ball. [With plates and plans.]* (monographic ed.). London: Longman & Co. Retrieved August 19, 2015, from https://flic.kr/p/hR5Ldx

Ball, N. (1891). *The pioneers of '49. A history of the excursion of the Society of California pioneers of New England.* Boston: Lee and Shepard. Retrieved August 19, 2015, from https://flic.kr/p/oujVou

Childs, J. L., & Collection, H. G. (1914). *Childs' Rare Flowers, Fruits and Vegetables.* Floral Park, New York: John Lewis Childs. Retrieved August 19, 2015, from https://flic.kr/p/x7zYkp

Crabtre, A. D. (1874). *The funny side of physic : or, The mysteries of medicine, presenting the humorous and serious sides of medical practice. An exposé of medical humbugs, quacks, and charlatans in all ages and all countries.* Hartford, The J. B. Burr publishing co. Retrieved August 19, 2015, from https://flic.kr/p/oeVnbp

Elton, (1854). *The Ball of Yarn.* New York: P. J. Cozans. Retrieved August 19, 2015, from https://flic.kr/p/owduBo

Goodrich, S. G. (1845). *Dick Boldhero : or, A tale of adventures in South America.* Philedelphia: Sorin and Ball. Retrieved August 19, 2015, from https://flic.kr/p/ovozA6

H.W. Koerner, Koerner, H. W., & Henry G. Gilbert Nursery & Seed Trade Catalog. (1900). *Koerner's annual travelling agent of seeds, bulbs, plants, shrubs and vines.* Milwaukiee, Wisconsin: H.W. Koerner. Retrieved August 2015, 2015, from https://flic.kr/p/xhoAVj

Hooker, W. J. (1830-1833). *Botanical Miscellany.* London: J. Murray. Retrieved August 19, 2015, from https://flic.kr/p/w8NLeb

Horapollo, Cousin, J., Du Pre, G., & Ruelle, J. (1574). *Ori Apollinis Niliaci, De sacris Aegyptiorum notis, Aegyptiacè expressis : libri duo, iconibus illustrati, & aucti : nunc primùm in latinum ac gallicum sermonem conversi.* Parisiis : Apud Galeotum à Prato, & Ioannem Ruellium: Via Iacobaea. Retrieved August 19, 2015, from https://flic.kr/p/osLJxX

Jasper, J., & Pimgadie, M. (1912). *De inlandsche kunstnijverheid in Nederlandsch Indië.* 's-Gravenhage, Mouton & co. Retrieved August 19, 2015, from https://flic.kr/p/ouFg2H

Kipling, R., & Willeumier, G. (1895). *Van dieren en kinderen. Vertaling van Mevrouw Willeumier. Met platen. [Seven tales from "The Jungle Book" and "Wee Willie Winkie."]", "Selections.* Amsterdam. Retrieved August 19, 2015, from https://flic.kr/p/idMotW

Moore, J. W. (1884). *Picturesque Washington: pen and pencil sketches of its scenery, history, traditions, public and social life, with graphic descriptions of the Capitol and Congress, the White House, and the government departments.* Providence, J.A. & R.A. Reid. Retrieved August 19, 2015, from https://flic.kr/p/ow1W1U

Pollard, A. W., & Pollard, A. (1902). *Old picture books; with other essays on bookish subjects.* London: Methuen and Co. Retrieved August 19, 2015, from https://flic.kr/p/oydQ7H

Ricci, L. H., & Sara Anderson Galleries, Inc. (1915). *Illustrated catalogue of rare and beautiful Sixteenth and Seventeenth century laces collected during twenty years by Leone Ricci, Esq. of Florence.* New York: Metropolitan Art Association. Retrieved August 19, 2015, from https://flic.kr/p/od6CgP

Sears, Roebuck and Co. (1916). *Wall Paper for Every Home, 1916.* Sears, Roebuck and Co. Retrieved August 19, 2015, from https://flic.kr/p/ovQuvH

W, B., & Mulready, W. (1883). *The Elephant's Ball and Grand Fete Champetre. [In verse.] Intended as companion to those much admired pieces, The Butterfly's Ball, and The Peacock "at home." Illustrated with elegant engravings [by William Mulready].* ([Another edition.] A facsimile reproduction of the edition of 1807. With an introduction by Charles Welsh. ed.). London: Griffith & Farran. Retrieved August 19, 2015, from https://flic.kr/p/ic86Qp

Washburn & Co, & Henry G. Gilbert Nursery and Seed Trade Catalog Co. (1869). *Washburn & Co.'s amateur cultivator's guide to the flower and kitchen garden : containing a descriptive list of two thousand varieties of flower and vegetable seeds : also a list of French hybrid gladiolus,.* Boston: The Company. Retrieved Augsut 19, 2015, from https://flic.kr/p/oeRZtT

IT'S A YORKIE LIFE

It's a Yorkie Life is a community of Yorkie Lovers big and small.

Join us on our
Website www.itsayorkielife.com,
Facebook http://facebook.com/itsayorkielife,
Pinterest http://pinterest.com/itsayorkielife or
Twitter http://twitter.com/itsayorkielife.

www.ingramcontent.com/pod-product-compliance
Lightning Source LLC
Chambersburg PA
CBHW080851170526
45158CB00009B/2705